This book belongs to:

Elephants can live for up to 70 years.

Their trunks are amazing. They use their trunks to smell, breathe, drink, grab things, and trumpet. They are also incredibly strong and flexible, capable of lifting heavy objects and picking up small items.

They can also smell predators from a distance, such as lions, and take precautions. Smell is also crucial in social interactions. They can recognize each other, and males can also smell the status of a female to determine if she is ready for mating

The skin of elephants is really thick, around 1 inch (2.5 centimeters) in most places. The wrinkles and folds on their skin can contain up to 10 times more water than flat skin, which really helps them cool down more on hot days.

They also use low-pitched noises that are nearly inaudible to humans to transmit messages across great distances. Other elephants experience these noises through their feet and bones as seismic vibrations and infrasonic rumbles in the atmosphere. Up to two miles can be covered by these messages.

Around 90 percent of elephants have been wiped out in the past century, particularly in Africa. The primary cause is the ivory trade, which involves illegally killing elephants for their tusks, made of ivory. It is estimated that around 415,000 African elephants still live in the wild today, along with approximately 50,000 elephants in Asia.

The elephant herd is led by the oldest and most experienced female elephant. She guides the herd by making decisions about migration, foraging, and protection. The herd usually consists of other females with their offspring.

The gestation period for a mother elephant is 22 months. That means she carries the baby for that long before giving birth. This is the longest gestation period of any land animal.

Elephants are very social animals. The mother teaches her little one how to behave and interact with other members and also about how to find food and survive in the wild. Other females in the group also help with raising the little one.

Young elephants are really playful by nature. They like to explore, swim, take mud baths, and play with each other.

Elephants can remember the faces of humans they have encountered for several years. If somebody harms an elephant, they will remember it. This also demonstrates their remarkable memory ability.

Elephants also have tails. The tail is relatively short compared to their body, but it still serves a purpose. The tail is equipped with hairs at the tip, which the elephant can use to ward off insects. Additionally, it serves as a communication tool.

PWe would bee deeply grateful for any kind of feedback in a review.

Thank u.

Anamarie Larik Publishing

Made in the USA
Las Vegas, NV
28 November 2024

12831298R00046